From Powerlessness to Possibility,
Life with an Ostomy

Stanley and Me make three

Jayne Prescott

From Powerlessness to Possibility,
Life with an Ostomy
Stanley and Me make three

TATE PUBLISHING
AND ENTERPRISES, LLC

This book is designed to provide accurate and authoritative information with regard to the subject matter covered. This information is given with the understanding that neither the author nor Tate Publishing, LLC is engaged in rendering legal, professional advice. Since the details of your situation are fact dependent, you should additionally seek the services of a competent professional.

The opinions expressed by the author are not necessarily those of Tate Publishing, LLC.

Published by Tate Publishing & Enterprises, LLC
127 E. Trade Center Terrace | Mustang, Oklahoma 73064 USA
1.888.361.9473 | www.tatepublishing.com

Tate Publishing is committed to excellence in the publishing industry. The company reflects the philosophy established by the founders, based on Psalm 68:11,
"The Lord gave the word and great was the company of those who published it."

Published in the United States of America

ISBN: 978-1-63449-942-2
1. Biography & Autobiography / Personal Memoirs
2. Biography & Autobiography / Medical
15.04.28

*This book is dedicated to my
superhero husband Michael and to all of the past, present,
and future ostomates. May we continue to have the
courage and the passion to
never give up.*

Contents

Preface

My illness was both a medical journey and a spiritual one. Unexplained sickness and physical decline are like a deep, dark hole where one falls. Some climb out and others are swallowed up by the experience and disappear. I quote biblical verses throughout this piece as these verses have always been a source of comfort to me. The words gave me hope and strength, and my mission is to share that power with you.

This is not a religious book, just a gift to those who are living, or attempting to come to terms with, life on life's terms. Know that there are those individuals out there who have experienced similar situations and have been able to conquer those fears and live a fulfilling, happy life. Hope is the antidote for fear.

You are not alone.

Jayne

Introduction

My name is Jayne, and I had to have a life-saving colorectal surgery in March 2013. The surgery prevented my colon from perforating, basically falling apart, and passing deadly poisons throughout my body and killing me. It ultimately saved my life, and it also changed my life forever. The surgery wasn't something that I wanted to have, but it was something that I had to have in order to survive. Here is a story about my new friend and ostomy, Lord Master Stanislaus, better known as...*Stanley*.

From Powerlessness to Possibility,
Life with an ostomy...
Stanley and Me make three.

1

The Onset

If God be for us, who can be against us?

—Romans 8:31

September 2012

I had just completed my master of business administration degree. Life was so great. I celebrated my accomplishment by vacationing for a week at the New Jersey shore, devouring succulent seafood dinners by night and eating gooey boardwalk pizza by day. When I returned to work and back to reality, I presented a proposal to my employer for a promotion and a few days later, began to bleed from my rectum once again.

Before we go any further, let's flashback to November 2011…

I went to a gastroenterologist due to slight blood in my bowel movement and stomach aches and pains. Chalking it up to stress, graduate studies, work presentations, and life challenges, my worries about the blood were minimal. I scheduled a colonoscopy at the doctor's request and was diagnosed with mild ulcerative colitis. I was told that it was not severe and could be managed with medication. Little did I know about flares and inflammatory bowel disease (IBD).

Up to this point in my life, my health was very good. Cholesterol level was low, blood pressure within normal range, blood work perfect, and weight fine. I was forty-eight years old, charged and ready to take on the world, and to see blood in the toilet after going number two was concerning.

Flares are basically flare-ups of the disease. Some people experience blood in their stool like I did, severe abdominal pain, urgent episodes of diarrhea, fever, dehydration, and many different combinations of these symptoms. Interestingly, not every person with bowel disease presents the same way. The disease is very individual...what I experienced is not necessarily what someone else will experience.

I was hospitalized seven times between the months of October 2012 and March 2013. I lost over thirty pounds of weight, bottoming out at a mere ninety-five pounds. Not being a large person, the weight loss was very noticeable. I looked like one of those photographs of a World War II Holocaust work camp survivor, skin over bone, all teeth, and sunken eyes. I was literally starving to death.

Each time I was hospitalized, it seemed that my prognosis worsened. My health declined to the point where I needed many blood transfusions, and eventually, TPN in order to live. TPN is total parenteral nutrition which is liquid nutrition administered through a central line, commonly a peripherally inserted central catheter or (PICC) line. My site was located on my upper right arm in one of the large veins. I had to learn how to set up the TPN pump, connecting all of the tubes together with an intravenous (IV) bag of nutrition every evening. The pump ran for twelve hours each night, slowly feeding my body the proper nutrients and giving me strength.

2

The Holidays

Thanksgiving 2012, I was in the hospital receiving powerful medications as my holiday feast, and drugs to treat ulcerative colitis which ultimately failed me. The Christmas holiday was celebrated at home, sleeping on the sofa due to nausea and weakness. New Year's Eve was celebrated in bed once again because of extreme exhaustion, perfuse diarrhea, and stabbing stomach pains.

People have asked me what it felt like to be sick with ulcerative colitis. Everyone is different, but my symptoms reminded me of having the flu with an intense intestinal bug. I often had a fever and was dehydrated due to the uncontrolled diarrhea. My bottom hurt too from all of the bathroom episodes…ouch!!!!

New Year's Day 2013, I managed to visit with my family for about two hours but could not enjoy the evening because I had awful abdominal pain and was very dehydrated. By mid-January, an emergency readmission to the hospital for ten days revealed that my health was declining so rapidly and that colorectal surgery was my destiny. The month of March was when I had to have the life-saving, life-altering ileostomy surgery.

3

Treatment and Transformation

This unfamiliar journey was a difficult one. As a type-A personality, very prepared and organized, I was not ready for this new "life normal." And to make matters more stressful, I did not know anyone with an ileostomy, colostomy, or urostomy. I truly believed that if I followed doctor's orders to the tee, not deviating from what the experts prescribed, I would get better. But I was still sick and getting worse every day. My body was failing me, and I could not understand why. Call me naïve, but I did not fully understand the ostomy or the chronic illness situation. The medical system quickly became my advocate and my mentor. I wanted my healthy, happy life back, and it was not happening. Why, why, why, why me…what a stressful, frightening experience!

I repeated these words often as a source of comfort and strength…

> I can do all things through Christ which strengtheneth me. (Philippians 4:13)

And I was lead to my brilliant colorectal surgeon. He had all of the pieces of the pre-surgery, surgery, and post-surgery puzzle in place for me. I also met with a wound care ostomy nurse to determine the best place or sight for my new, permanent stoma.

What is a stoma? I thought. I quickly learned that it is a surgical opening made on the belly where waste, bowel movement or "effluent" as the medical community refers to it, is secreted. I had to wear a pouch twenty-four hours a day, seven days a week on the right side of my stomach to catch the waste material. Oh boy…I had heard all these scary stories about "the bag." Now I was the one going to be holding the bag and stuck with it forever.

The position of the stoma is very important because you do not want an appliance malfunction or basically leaks. My stoma sits just below my belly button, slightly to the right. When the wound care nurse and I selected the position, I sat down, bent over, and moved all around with an appliance sample stuck to my belly. I did this to make certain that the position was comfortable for me and the appliance did not peel off like an adhesive bandage when I moved. When surgery is an emergency, a stoma sight is selected by the surgeon and this process is not possible.

The words "what was happening to me" raced through my mind every minute of every day. I could not comprehend how this was going to be a successful, positive experience, although all the doctors and nurses assured me that I would be just fine.

4

The New Way

For I the Lord thy God will hold thy
right hand, saying unto thee,
Fear not; I will help thee

—Isaiah 41:13

My surgery went very well. According to my surgeon, the operation was 100 percent successful. I was perfect. But was I really?

The surgery was performed laproscopically, meaning I had several small incisions on my belly rather than a long incision beginning from my belly button straight down to my pelvic area. All this equated to less recovery time because there was less trauma to my body. The surgeon also closed up my backside or anus. I now have a Barbie butt. If only I looked like a Barbie doll.

I was in the hospital for five nights and discharged on the sixth day. My surgeon wanted to discharge me earlier, but I begged and pleaded with him to allow me stay the extra day because I was terrified to go home and face this "stoma" and bag on my own. I was melting down, drenched with fear.

Fortunately, my wonderful husband Michael was by my side. He was my cornerstone, my rock for the duration. Michael was there helping me to cope with my "new normal" and throughout the entire recovery process. Everybody needs a Michael in their life, a steadfast friend, to reassure them that all will be okay. He continues to encourage me, giving me the confidence to face each day with guts and determination.

I want you to know that in the very beginning, the first few weeks after surgery were very scary and anxiety driven. I was frightened of everything, and due to these fears, I was unable to sleep. I worried all the time, and thought that this surgery, gaining a stoma, was, after the fact, a very bad idea. I could not appreciate in those early days what my stoma gave me...precious quality of life. Better yet...life itself.

5

Meeting Stanley

This is how Stanley was born. I named my stoma so I could develop a relationship with this funny-looking thing. The good, the bad, and the poopy… Stanley and I were in this together so we had to become best buddies. Really, he had already bonded with me, but I was extremely resistant. In the beginning, I treated my stoma like some foreign object—a small, damp thing sticking out of my belly. Today, he is just part of the daily routine—he is me and I am him.

Wow…in the early days, Stanley made lots of funny sounds. He tooted, blew bubbles, whistled, and quacked like a duck. And he continues to blow raspberries on me fairly often, and it feels funny on my skin. I've accepted that Stanley has a lot to say at the most inopportune moments. For example, when I am trying to sleep, he is chattering away. I sometimes refer to his behavior as percolating.

Maintaining the pouch and appliance was tricky in the beginning. A medical wafer with a strong adhesive is cut to the stoma size, placed over the stoma, and secured to the stomach. Arts and crafts were never my strong suite, but after several lessons from the wound care nurse about cutting the wafer and securing a good fit, the change became less daunting. Several medical device companies also provided informational CDs and literature for review. These guides were helpful and educational, and I soaked up the information like a sponge.

6

Living the New Normal

> And we know that all things work
> together for good to them that love God,
> to them who are the called according
> to his purpose.
>
> —Romans 8:28

Since having the surgery, Stanley and I have enjoyed many events. Going out to dinner and eating a variety of foods is one favorite. Once more, Caesar salads, beef tenderloin, spaghetti and meatballs, yummy nachos with extra sour cream, and soft pretzels grace our carte du jour. Stanley is very happy digesting our much-loved foods and, in his own special way, thanks me for those nutritional delights. A friend shared that in some cultures, belching is a compliment to the chef. Stanley is very polite and complimentary.

What lessens these highly vocal moments is eating meals at fairly regular times, limiting carbonated beverages, and keeping track of the foods that cause the most music. Fortunately, I am able to eat most things that I enjoyed prior to surgery. I do chew my food more thoroughly, eat more slowly, and drink additional beverage because it was recommended to do so by the medical staff to help with digestion.

Colorectal surgery continues to have a dark, hush-hush stigma, but I cannot allow it to define me. I am who I am, pouch and all, colon and colon-less. If I do not confide in others about my surgery, no one would ever notice the change in my bodily appearance. Society seems to be afraid to talk about bathroom issues and the lack of control that may come along with bowel disease. How can I be ashamed of something that I had simply no control?

As an additional support, local ostomy support meetings, conferences, and online groups are freely available. These get-togethers are so much fun and extremely important. The groups educate and connect others experiencing a similar journey. I've met people, my brothers and sisters from other mothers and misters, who have been successfully living with an ostomy, sometimes two ostomies, for many years. We are not alone.

7

The Three of Us

As the days tick by, Mike and I continue to celebrate our new lease on life running around and most of all, having lots of fun. We recently attended a Philadelphia Phillies baseball game, and Stanley was singing "Take Me Out to the Ball Game" in his own special way. My belly is not as distended from the surgery as it once was, and I wear the majority of my old clothing from the pre-surgery days. I also gained most of the weight back that I lost during my five-month ulcerative colitis flare. I am back to me again.

Ironically, Stanley and I were always together... whether he was on the inside or on the outside. Stanley and Mike saved my life and will be forever grateful for the second chance. I never wanted Stanley to be part of my day-to-day activities as three is considered a crowd. Let's admit, Stanley was always there...like the silent, or not so silent, partner.

Being sick taught me a valuable lesson... live each day to the fullest extent possible because today may be the last. Without Stanley, my stoma,

Mike and I would not be able to experience a warm sunny day, a mysterious full moon, the aroma of fresh cut grass, a morning walk on the beach as the waves melt along the sand, a crisp autumn day, a gentle snow, or better yet, delicious, glorious food.

By choosing the gift of life, I had to accept and embrace a stoma. Lord Master Stanislaus took some getting used to, and still does at times, but I do appreciate my little intestine and the functions that he performs. Life goes on and continues beautifully.

Thank God for Mike and thank God for Stanley. What a wonderful, winning team the three of us make.

Appendix

Ostomy Resources and Reference Guide

The United Ostomy Associations of America, Inc. – www.ostomy.org

Meet an Ostomate – www.meetanostomate.org

Ostomy Product Distributors

McKesson Patient Care Solutions, LLC – 888-202-5700

American Ostomy Supply – 800-858-5858

Bruce Medical Supply – 800-225-8446
Byram Healthcare – 877-902-9726
Edgepark Medical Supplies– 888-394-5375
Express Medical Supply – 800-633-2139
Liberator Medical Supply – 888-653-3150
Medical Care Products – 800-741-0110
Ostomy Care Supply – 866-207-5909
The Parthenon Company, Inc. – 800-453-8898
SGV Medical Supplies– 800-395-6099
Shield HealthCare – 800-765-8775
Total eMedical –877-750-5252

Ostomy Product Manufacturers
ColoPlast
ConvaTec
Genairex
Hollister Incorporated
NB Products – Na'Scent Ostomy deodorant
Marlen Manufacturing
Nu-Hope Laboratories

Ostomy Secrets

Ostaway x-Bag

Torbot

The Phoenix Magazine, the official publication of the UOAA, provides answers to the many challenges of living with an ostomy.

Disclaimer: No suggestions made, or any products named in this publication, are considered to be an endorsement. This is information for the ostomates, caregivers, friends, and interested individuals. Always consult your doctor and/or wound care nurse before using any ostomy management products or procedures.

Thank you for reading about my medical journey. I look forward to seeing you at a conference or a support group sometime.

References

"Jack Norworth & Take Me Out to the Ball Game."
Laguna Beach Historical Society. Archived
from the original on February 4, 2008.
Retrieved 2014, November 17 Wikipedia.

Barbie is a Fashion doll manufactured by
the American toy-company Mattel, Inc.
and launched in March 1959. American
businesswoman Ruth Handler is credited
with the creation of the doll using a German
doll called Bild Lilli as her inspiration.
Retrieved 2015, March 16 Wikipedia.

Made in the USA
San Bernardino, CA
13 December 2016